RELIEF FROM IBS

*Simple steps for
long term control of
irritable bowel syndrome*

D1099459

RELIEF FROM IBS

*Simple steps for
long-term control of
irritable bowel syndrome*

VERNON COLEMAN

EUROPEAN MEDICAL JOURNAL

First published in 1995 by the European Medical Journal, PO Box 30,
Barnstaple, Devon EX32 9YU

The recipes in this book first appeared in *Eat Green – Lose Weight,* by
Vernon Coleman

ISBN   0 898947 03 1

A catalogue record for this book is available from the British Library

Printed and bound in England by Biddles Ltd., Guildford and King's Lynn

CONTENTS

Note

Visit your doctor before following the advice in this book. He may be able to help you. Many doctors do now recognise how troublesome the irritable bowel syndrome can be. Do not make the diagnosis yourself. You must let your doctor make the diagnosis. If your doctor diagnoses irritable bowel syndrome, ask him/her to confirm that you can safely follow the advice in this book.

PREFACE

I FIRST WROTE about the irritable bowel syndrome back in the mid 1980s when the disorder was virtually unheard of by doctors and patients alike. I was staggered by the response. I quickly realised that millions of people were suffering from this troublesome, exhausting and sometimes life ruining disorder but that their doctors, for one reason or another, either failed to diagnose the condition or had taken little interest in offering any treatment. Many of these patients spent months or in some cases years wandering from doctor to doctor and hospital to hospital. Some had countless uncomfortable examinations. Not a few had repeated surgery in an attempt to deal with a problem which just wouldn't go away.

It became clear to me that although the irritable bowel syndrome produces very real physical symptoms there is no clearly definable underlying physical abnormality. The disease is difficult to diagnose and difficult to treat. When to those two facts you add the fact that the disease tends to persist for years it isn't difficult to see why doctors weren't taking much interest. Doctors much prefer treating easily defined problems for which they can prescribe a handful of pills or a surgical procedure. The irritable bowel syndrome is a confusing hotch potch of symptoms. There is no single cause. There is no single treatment.

As I studied the syndrome and it became obvious that

the condition affected millions — not thousands — of patients I was, for a while, puzzled by the fact that the condition seemed to have arrived out of nowhere. Could there, I wondered, be a modern explanation for this apparently modern disease?

And then I realised that the syndrome has been around for decades. But it wasn't always called the irritable bowel syndrome. Back in the past it was known by various other names — including spastic colon.

The dramatic rise in the incidence of the disorder is simply a result of our changing lifestyle. We eat packaged, highly refined foods which are rich in fat and sugar. We don't do much exercise. And we expose ourselves to constant stresses and strains.

Irritable bowel syndrome is not a disorder which can be permanently eradicated. If you are prone to these symptoms then you will probably always be susceptible if you re-expose yourself to the factors which were originally responsible for their development. You should always regard any vague, faint symptom of trouble as a sign that you need to take better care of yourself.

My interest in the irritable bowel syndrome became more than academic or professional when I realised that I too was a victim. My search for the truth about this disabling disorder was consequently nourished by my own pain and my own fears. This book contains the advice and information I acquired and used myself. I hope you find it as effective as I have.

Vernon Coleman
Devon 1994

FOREWORD

FOR SEVERAL MONTHS I had a persistent, nagging pain in my back. It was just about in the region of my right kidney. It didn't seem to be getting any worse but it certainly wasn't getting any better.

For a while I managed to convince myself that it was nothing more than a muscular backache caused by crouching over a typewriter.

But then I noticed two additional symptoms.

I started feeling constantly 'full' — as though I had just eaten a large meal — and I found myself visiting the lavatory more often than I found entirely convenient.

When I told my general practitioner he took a routine urine sample.

And found blood.

The next step was a hospital appointment.

The ultrasound pictures showed a rather mis-shapen kidney. And more specialist X-ray pictures confirmed that there was something wrong. My kidney looked as though it was auditioning for a part as the hunchback of Notre Dame.

Unhappily, however, the radiologists couldn't get a really good view of my kidney. Their view was obscured by large bubbles of inconvenient gas lurking around in the coiled nooks and crannies of my intestinal loops.

So I was given an appointment to go to another, larger,

city hospital for even more sophisticated tests. It was all very worrying. I knew that the doctors who had examined me suspected the worst. And without anyone saying anything I knew exactly how bad the worst could be. Very bad.

I breathed a huge sigh of relief when the kindly radiologist at the large city hospital told me that there was nothing seriously wrong with my kidney. It was, he assured me, mis-shapen but perfectly healthy.

And so, after racing up to Bristol to record a couple of TV programmes, and hurtling back home to write a column, I set off, as I had previously planned, to Paris.

On the plane flying over the Channel the pain in my back got much, much worse.

And I suddenly realised what was wrong.

The gas that the radiologist had spotted in my intestines had expanded because of the change in air pressure and it was the gas that was causing my pain.

But it was, I suddenly realised, the gas that was also making me feel 'full' all the time.

And irritating my bowel and my bladder.

And pressing on my kidney and causing the bleeding.

There was only one explanation for this apparently bizarre set of circumstances.

I had irritable bowel syndrome.

The moment I made the diagnosis I realised just why I had acquired this most common of twentieth-century disorders.

First, I had been putting myself under an enormous amount of stress. For years I had run a series of passionate campaigns designed to spread the truth and oppose those parts of the medical establishment with which I disagreed. I had, for years, been spending at least twelve hours a day on my campaigns.

Second, I had changed my diet. When I had, a few years earlier, decided to become a vegetarian I had cut out meat and fish and increased the quantity of vegetables and cereals. I had also started eating a lot of cheese and cheese based dishes. When in a rush I would make myself a cheese sandwich for lunch.

In order to control my irritable bowel syndrome I had to learn to control my exposure to stress (and my own reaction to the inevitable stress in my life) and I had to learn to change my diet again.

Eventually, after much trial and error, I succeeded in making the changes which brought my irritable bowel syndrome under control. And the techniques I discovered and developed really do work. I don't believe that irritable bowel syndrome can be cured (in the same way that a broken leg can be cured) because the weakness and susceptibility will remain. The symptoms of irritable bowel syndrome still trouble me occasionally — but *only* if I have eaten unwisely or been under an unusual amount of stress and even then they are not as severe as they were before.

This book contains the information I used to help myself deal with my symptoms. I hope and believe that the advice and information I've accumulated will also help you.

WHAT IS THE IRRITABLE BOWEL SYNDROME?

THE IRRITABLE BOWEL syndrome (IBS) is one of the commonest and most troublesome of all diseases. Some experts claim that at one time or another as many as one in three people suffer from it. It affects men as much as women — although it is usually regarded as a disease which primarily affects young women in their twenties, thirties and forties — and it affects the young as much as the old. Children under ten can get it and there are many sufferers in their seventies and eighties.

IBS probably affects as many people as toothache or the common cold.

It is also one of the most commonly misdiagnosed of all diseases — and one of the most badly treated. Once it has developed it hardly ever disappears completely.

That's the bad news.

The good news is twofold.

First, irritable bowel syndrome isn't dangerous or life threatening; it doesn't turn into anything more serious, it won't turn into cancer and it won't kill you or even threaten your life.

The symptoms associated with irritable bowel syndrome may be exhausting, irritating, worrying and disabling but there does not usually seem to be any underlying pathology.

And second, although it does tend to persist — once you have got it you've probably got it for life — IBS can be controlled. There is no quick, simple, reliable cure because there is no clearly defined cause. But although you may not be able to conquer irritable bowel syndrome completely — and make the symptoms disappear — you *can* control it.

Not many sufferers have less than three of the symptoms I'm about to describe — symptoms which I am going to group into categories simply for the sake of convenience.

The symptoms

First, there are the primary symptoms which involve the bowel itself and what goes on inside it. Pain is probably the most obvious of these symptoms — though it is also one of the most variable. It is often a colicky, spasmodic sort of pain which comes and goes in waves; it can affect just about any part of the abdomen and it frequently fades a little when the sufferer goes to the toilet.

Bowel irregularities are common too.

Most sufferers complain of diarrhoea — which can sometimes be quite sudden and explosive — but, oddly enough, constipation is also a common symptom. Sometimes the two problems alternate. There may also be the passage of some mucus.

The third very common bowel problem associated with this complaint is wind and this really is typical. Most sufferers complain that their tummies swell up so much that their clothes don't fit them properly. Many complain of embarrassing rumblings and gurglings and other noises and of the social problems associated with escaping wind.

A published survey of IBS sufferers showed that every single patient with this problem complained of these three symptoms: abdominal pain, abdominal distension caused by wind and an abnormal bowel habit.

Next, there are the secondary physical symptoms which affect a lot of sufferers but which don't affect all patients. You're almost certain to have the three primary symptoms but you are unlikely to have all of these secondary symptoms.

One or two of the secondary symptoms are caused by the wind that is so widely associated with IBS and these will probably come and go as the wind comes and goes. Symptoms in this category include a feeling of being full all the time and not being able to eat very much; a constant feeling of nausea; heartburn; and indigestion. Back pains of one sort or another are also fairly commonplace and these too are frequently a result of wind accumulating in the intestines. It's even quite common for sufferers to complain of urinary frequency and other bladder problems caused by pressure produced by wind in the intestines.

Last, but certainly not least, there are the mental symptoms which aren't in any direct way related to the intestines or what is going on inside them. Anxiety, depression and irritability are all common but the one mental symptom that really seems more common than any other is tiredness.

Even though you may be quite convinced that you are suffering from the irritable bowel syndrome you shouldn't make the diagnosis by yourself without visiting your doctor. Although IBS is probably the commonest of all bowel problems today, there are other problems which can cause bowel symptoms and only by visiting your doctor can you be absolutely sure that you have got the diagnosis right.

The causes

There are, I believe, two main causes of IBS.

The first is stress.

I know that the word 'stress' has been used a lot in the last few years. And you may feel that it has been over-worked. But the plain fact is that all muscles can be tightened up when you are under too much stress. Tension headaches are a good example of what happens when the muscles around your head are tightened by worry and anxiety. The muscles in your bowel walls are no exception — they are as vulnerable and as susceptible to stress as any other muscles — and in some individuals it is these muscles which suffer first when stress starts to get out of control. Lots of people who don't suffer from the irritable bowel syndrome do get diarrhoea or cramping pains in their tummies when they are under too much pressure or when they are anxious.

The second explanation for the current epidemic of IBS lies in the type of food we tend to eat these days.

In the last century or so the people who produce, market and sell our food have changed our diet almost beyond recognition.

Today most of us eat a bland over-refined diet that contains very little natural roughage. And the result is that our bowels can't cope very well with this change — they haven't had time to adapt and so they struggle. Our grand-parents ate a diet that contained lots of raw, natural foods. We tend to live on prepackaged, convenience foods that may be rich in vitamins and minerals but which are dangerously short on fibre.

Although I do not believe that there is any single wonder cure for IBS, there are a good many ways in which you can control your symptoms.

First, I suggest that you take a good, hard look at the amount of stress in your life.

Try, for example, to make a list of all the things which worry you, which make you feel uptight, which keep you awake at night, which give you butterflies in your stomach or which you know upset you.

Try to decide what things are really important to you. Decide how you are going to allocate your time. And make sure that every week you take some time off.

If you want to relax properly you're going to have to work at it — and that will take a little effort and a little time. Learning to relax is like learning to drive a car or learning to play golf or learning to dance: you'll only get good at it if you put some effort into it. The advice in the second half of this book will help ensure that the adverse effect of stress on your body is kept to an absolute minimum.

Next, you probably need to take a long, cool, careful and critical look at your diet.

You will almost certainly benefit if you gradually increase the amount of fibre that you eat. I'll give you some detailed tips further on in the book but basically all you really have to do in order to increase your fibre intake is to start eating wholemeal bread or high bran cereals, wholewheat pasta, brown rice, oats — in porridge for example — and more fresh vegetables and fruit. Be careful, though, for if you suffer a lot from wind you will probably be wise to avoid any vegetables — such as sprouts — which seem to cause you a lot of wind. Try to get into the habit of nibbling fruit, seeds and, occasionally, nuts instead of chocolate and sweets.

I really think that most IBS sufferers will benefit from cutting down their fat intake too. If you eat meat then cut off the visible fat and avoid red meats as often as you can. Drink skimmed or semi skimmed milk rather than the full fat variety; buy low fat salad dressings and use single cream rather than double. Make low fat pastry, don't add fat when cooking and grill, bake, steam, poach, casserole and boil rather than roast or fry. When you make chips cut them thickly so that they soak up less fat and make sure that the fat is sizzling hot. Replace butter on vegetables with herbs and instead of butter on bread use a low fat spread. Once again, there are more detailed notes further on in the book.

Finally, try to do more exercise. Don't make the mistake of adding stress to your life by trying to run faster than anyone else or by trying to win the local tennis club trophy. But do try to take more exercise that is fun. Walk, swim, dance, cycle or work out in the gym — all those things will help you because gentle, regular exercise seems to have a soothing effect on the bowel.

THE TWO-STEP PROGRAMME FOR IBS CONTROL

Step 1
CHANGE WHAT YOU EAT AND THE WAY YOU EAT IT

The type of food you eat — and to a lesser extent how you eat it and when you eat it — will have a tremendous influence on the health of your bowel. The advice on the following pages is primarily designed to help keep your IBS under control but if you follow the advice I've given then there will be a bonus: you should find that other aspects of health are also improved. The low fat, low sugar, high fibre diet which seems to help reduce the symptoms will also help protect you against heart disease and some types of cancer.

1. CUT OUT ALL MILK, CHEESE AND DAIRY PRODUCE

I am quite convinced that many cases of IBS are caused or at the very least made worse by a reaction to milk and dairy produce. Your symptoms may not be caused by an allergy to dairy produce but you can obtain the nutrients which are available in dairy produce from other foods and I think it is well worth while cutting them out. If you're a genuine sufferer from IBS then you will, I suspect, readily agree that having to do without milk and cheese is a small price to pay for no IBS symptoms. If your symptoms clear up you can try reintroducing small quantities of milk or cheese to your diet later on. You can replace cow's milk with soya milk and yoghurt lovers will no doubt be pleased to know that it is possible to buy soya yoghurt too!

2. EAT MORE FIBRE

Most of us eat far too little fibre. For years now the food manufacturers have been removing fibre from food and throwing it away. The result is that we have been eating a diet for which our bodies were not designed. You will, I think, benefit enormously by following the advice below.

- Try to eat more bread. Your intake of fibre will be kept highest if you eat wholemeal rather than white bread.

- Eat more pasta. Again your intake of fibre will be maximised if you eat wholewheat pasta rather than white pasta.

- Make a real effort to eat more fresh vegetables, a simple move which will dramatically increase your fibre intake. Try not to peel vegetables before you cook them — and certainly don't peel them too thickly. Take special care not to cook your vegetables for too long. And make sure that you cook them in as little water as possible: best of all, steam them. When preparing salads, add shredded or grated raw vegetables.

- Increase your intake of fresh fruit. Most fruits are rich in fibre.

- Eat more rice. If possible eat brown rice rather than white rice.

- When you are cooking use wholemeal or wholewheat flour whenever possible.

- Oats are an excellent source of fibre. You can eat them in cereals or in porridge or you can use them to make biscuits and crumbles.

- Instead of nibbling sugar rich sweets or fat rich chocolates eat fibre rich dried fruits between meals when you want a snack.

- Try to eat more pulses (such as beans). These contain quite a lot of fibre.

- If you must buy biscuits (which tend to contain large quantities of sugar) try to buy wholemeal biscuits — which are likely to contain more fibre.

WARNING: you should increase the amount of fibre you eat fairly gradually and slowly. If you suddenly and dramatically increase your fibre intake you may suffer from wind, pain and other signs of abdominal discomfort.

3. EAT LESS SUGAR

Your body doesn't need sugar. Sugar will make you fat and it will rot your teeth. And I think that a diet which is rich in sugar will make your irritable bowel syndrome worse. Here are some simple ways in which you can make sure that you eat less sugar.

- Make an effort to reduce the amount of sugar you use in drinks such as tea or coffee. If you can't cope with hot drinks unless they are sweetened try using one of the many available artificial sweeteners. As an alternative try reducing the number of cups of tea or coffee that you drink or change to other types of hot drink (for example: tea with lemon or peppermint tea) which do not need sweetening.

- Don't buy sugar rich soft drinks. Instead choose low calorie drinks or mineral water.

- Eat more natural foods — and fewer prepackaged foods. Some foods (such as fruit) do contain natural sugars but these will be mixed with lots of fibre and will be far less likely to do you harm. If you buy tinned fruits, select those which are packed in their own juices rather than in a sugar rich syrup.

- Buy jams and marmalades which contain less sugar than usual and when baking experiment by using slightly less sugar than recipes recommend.

- When cooking try using spices or fruits to sweeten foods — instead of adding an enormous amount of sugar.

- Choose dried fruits and nuts for evening nibbling —

instead of buying sweets and chocolates. But watch out because some nuts contain a lot of fat.

- If you are spreading jam or marmalade on bread do it thinly to reduce your sugar intake.

- Avoid sugar and fat rich puddings and instead choose fresh fruit. Most restaurants will be able to serve you a piece of fruit even if their official 'sweet trolley' doesn't contain anything other than fat and sugar rich creations.

- Don't buy sweetened yoghurts. Buy natural, unsweetened yoghurt and add your own fruit in order to give the yoghurt the flavour you want. (I suggest that you buy soya yoghurt).

- When buying fruit juices look for the natural variety rather than the ones which have added sugar.

4. EAT LESS FAT

It is vitally important that you reduce the amount of fat in your diet. The tips which follow are important. As a bonus your diet will be much healthier. You will be far less likely to develop heart disease and less likely to develop some types of cancer.

- Don't fry or roast food. Grill, steam, poach, casserole, bake or boil — but don't fry or roast unless you absolutely must! If you do fry then use a non stick pan so that you don't have to add extra fat to whatever it is that you are cooking.

- If you drink cows' milk, use skimmed or semi skimmed milk rather than the full fat variety.

- Avoid butter and margarine (which contain a lot of saturated fat) and use low fat spreads instead. You will find it easier to be more sparing with fatty spreads if you make an effort to buy bread which you really like. Good bread doesn't need a layer of fat to make it palatable.

- If you must eat meat (which isn't good for your health) then eat only lean meat; avoid red meat whenever you can (because red meat is often rich in hidden or invisible fat); cut off visible fat before cooking or eating; and after grilling or cooking meat on a rack (so that the fat drips out) throw the fat away rather than try to find a use for it in the kitchen.

- Try to use liquid oil which is rich in polyunsaturates and which contains few saturates, instead of a hard fat, when you are baking.

CHANGE WHAT YOU EAT

- Add herbs rather than butter to vegetables when you have cooked them. Vegetables don't need to have butter added to them if they have been properly cooked.

- Try to use less fat in cooking. Experiment with low fat recipes.

- When making chips out of potatoes cut them thickly (because they will soak up less fat), make sure that the fat or oil you use is very hot before you add the chips (they will soak up less of the fat if it is very hot) and dry them on kitchen paper after you have cooked them in order to remove any excess oil.

- If you must buy cream buy single cream rather than double cream.

5. DRINK MORE WATER

You need to increase your fluid intake. But caffeine rich drinks (such as coffee or tea) and milk may make things worse. So I suggest that you drink more water. You should drink at least three litres a day.

If you have any doubts about the safety of your local water supply then buy (and use) a water filter or buy bottled water for drinking.

As a change and to give your drinking more flavour drink low calorie squashes.

I suggest that you try to limit yourself to no more than three cups of coffee or tea a day. Use low calorie sweeteners instead of sugar and if you add milk to hot drinks try to use soya milk or a powder which is not made from cow's milk.

Remember to drink plenty of fluid every day!

6. STOP EATING BIG MEALS

Eating three square meals a day is old fashioned and unhealthy.

It is also bad for you.

When you eat at fixed meal times you eat whether you are hungry or not. And because you and your body know that it will be some hours before you eat another big meal there is a tendency to overeat. This is bad for you in two main ways. First, the amount of food in a large meal puts a great strain on your digestive system. Second, your body will store the excess food as fat so that you can live off the fatty stores while you are not eating. But your next fixed meal time will probably come along just before your body starts burning up those fat stores and the result is that you will gain unnecessary weight.

By eating little and often — nibbling, snacking or 'grazing' — your health will benefit in many ways. And your IBS will be far less troublesome.

Eating at fixed meal times is, as far as your body is concerned, a bizarre, unnatural and thoroughly irrational way to eat. Your body doesn't just need food three times a day. It needs energy supplies all day long. By choosing to eat fixed meals you create problems for yourself. Meal times are not natural. They were invented because they just happen to fit in with the way most of us work and live. If you get most of your calories three times a day at fixed meal times then you are almost certain to end up over-weight. Calories that aren't burnt up straight away will end up stuck on your hips. And however much you try to diet the chances are that you will fail.

Here are three reasons why you should never eat another meal again:

1   When you eat at fixed meal times you eat whether you are hungry or not. Instead of obeying your body's inbuilt appetite control centre you eat because the clock shows that it is time to eat. Your body's internal appetite control can make sure that you never get fat — if only you let it. But eating meals at fixed meal times means that your natural appetite control centre doesn't get a chance to work properly.

2   When you eat at fixed meal times you tend to eat what is available, what you have prepared or what you have been given — whether you need it or not. It is easy to eat the wrong foods — and to eat too much.

3   Because you and your body know that it will be some hours before you eat another big meal there is a tendency to overeat.

While you're changing your eating habits you should also make a real effort to eat *less*. Most of us eat far too much — dangerously overloading our bodies!

Every time you are about to eat ask yourself if you are genuinely hungry. If you are — then eat! But as soon as your hunger has gone — stop eating!

What can you eat?

Don't be worried or puzzled about what you can eat — and how you can eat a balanced diet without eating meals. Here are some MINI-MEAL suggestions to give you one or two ideas! I suggest that you devise your own mealettes and give up big, stodgy meals for ever!

1. Mixed vegetable soup
2. Baked beans on wholemeal toast

3. Raw carrot with dip
4. Small herb omelette
5. Tomato salad
6. Low fat soya yoghurt
7. Boiled egg with slice of bread
8. Raw apple
9. Salad sandwich on wholemeal bread
10. Slice melon
11. Bowl of porridge
12. Corn on the cob
13. Vegetable pasty
14. Half a grapefruit
15. Bowl of cornflakes with soya milk
16. Fresh fruit salad
17. Spaghetti with tomato sauce
18. Baked potato (small) with cole slaw and pineapple
19. Grilled vegetable burger in bun
20. Two toasted muffins with honey
21. Orange
22. Tomato soup
23. Hot French croissant
24. Toasted tea cake
25. Baked potato with baked beans
26. Pitta bread with salad filling
27. Rice with nuts and raisins
28. Pear
29. Banana on wholemeal bread sandwich
30. Leek soup
31. Fried mushrooms
32. Bowl of muesli
33. Humous and cucumber sandwich
34. Chopped raw vegetable platter
35. Stir fry vegetables

36. Dessert whip made with soya milk
37. Mushroom soup
38. Egg and chips
39. Avocado pear
40. Digestive biscuits
41. Crunchy cereal bar
42. Egg and cress sandwich
43. Asparagus soup
44. Two plums
45. Soya ice cream

These MINI-MEALS are not offered as part of a recommended diet but simply as an example of possible mealettes.

Warning

Remember that you should always check with your doctor before changing your diet — particularly if you are undergoing treatment of any kind or are not in the best of health.

If you are going to start the MINI-MEAL diet then you must *stop* eating meals. You can't eat MINI-MEALS and ordinary meals as well!

You don't have to be unsociable and leave your family and friends to eat alone. If they want a meal, sit down with them, but just eat a snack.

7. GET RID OF THE WIND

Wind is, after the common cold, the second most common disorder known to modern women and men. It is a well known problem among IBS sufferers. Many complain that they become so bloated that sometimes they cannot wear their own clothes!

Fortunately many eminent medical practitioners have for years devoted much time and effort to the study of this always delicate, often noisy, sometimes malodorous and invariably embarrassing problem.

If you suffer from persistent or recurrent wind then you should, of course, go and see your doctor for personal advice. But if he is unable to help you and an examination shows no abnormality then there may still be things that you can do to help yourself.

Here are some fairly simple to follow, straightforward tips designed to help you deal with wind both effectively and, I hope, permanently.

1   Try to limit the amount of air that you swallow. I know this probably sounds very obvious but two thirds of the gas in your body is probably swallowed air. You're likely to swallow too much air if you eat too quickly, gulp hot drinks or sip drinks through a straw. Habits like chewing gum, smoking, and sucking mints can also cause wind to accumulate. Chewing with an open mouth or talking with your mouth full increase the likelihood of wind too. Loose dentures can make wind worse — again by encouraging the swallowing of air.

2   Avoid the sort of foods that are likely to cause wind.

Specific foods that are likely to cause problems include: beans, broccoli, cabbage, raisins, bananas, popcorn, peanuts, onions, chocolate, coffee and milk. Fizzy drinks are an obvious cause of wind. And although high fibre diets are very fashionable they can be a cause of wind in a lot of people so watch out — you may need to reduce your intake of fibre if you constantly suffer from wind. This may mean eating white bread instead of wholemeal bread, white pasta instead of wholemeal pasta and avoiding the skins of potatoes and other vegetables and fruits. Fibre is good for you but in excess can result in painful wind.

3 Make sure that you avoid getting constipated. Constipation does seem to be a common cause of wind. Make sure that you don't eat too many starchy, stodgy foods and do try to keep your fluid intake up — water and fruit juices are ideal.

4 If the wind builds up try changing position — try sitting down, standing up, lying down or walking about. You might find that lying down in a warm bath helps.

5 Some sufferers find that sweets containing peppermint may help — others swear by peppermint tea.

6 Charcoal biscuits — usually obtainable from health stores — sometimes seem to help.

7 Watch out for tight clothing — it may make things worse.

8 Posture when eating is quite important. If you lean over a low table (or lean forward) when eating, you may suffer more from wind.

8. EAT ONLY WHAT YOUR BODY NEEDS

Learn to listen to your stomach and to get into the habit of eating when you are hungry rather than just because the clock tells you that it is time to eat. Your appetite control centre is designed to control your eating habits quite accurately.

A study published in the *American Journal of Diseases of Children* some years ago showed that when newly weaned infants just a few months old were allowed to choose what they ate from a range of simple, natural foods they selected balanced diets which were just as good in nutritional value as the carefully balanced ideal diets worked out by nutritional experts.

Another study published in the *Journal of the American Dental Association* showed that young children automatically choose foods that enable them to avoid digestive upsets and constipation.

A third study, done on soldiers during the Second World War, showed that when allowed access to unlimited supplies of food, troops ate what their bodies needed according to the outside temperature and automatically chose an ideal mixture of protein, fat and carbohydrate.

Unfortunately, most of us have lost the art of listening to our own bodies and we tend to eat three meals a day whether we are hungry or not, stuffing our bodies with food not because we need it but because the clock says it is time to eat. In practice the stomach does not adapt well to huge meals at lengthy intervals and it can cope far more effectively with smaller meals taken at shorter intervals.

We've also lost the art of knowing when we've had enough to eat.

Most of us make the mistake of always finishing the food on our plates because we've been trained that wasting food is wrong.

Your digestive system will be much healthier (and far less likely to succumb to stress) if you re-establish control of your appetite control centre by eating when you feel hungry, stopping when you feel full — and nibbling smaller meals more frequently rather than stuffing yourself with large meals occasionally.

9. LOOK AFTER YOUR DIGESTIVE SYSTEM

Most of us have a weak point. Some people get headaches when they are under pressure. Others get asthma, heart pains, diarrhoea or skin rashes. The human body, like most complex pieces of machinery, doesn't go all wrong at once. There is usually one part that is weaker than the rest.

If you are a regular sufferer from IBS, the chances are that your digestive system is your weak point. You can do a lot to look after your digestive system and to keep it happy and healthy.

Follow these simple rules for better eating habits:

1 Eat slowly. People often stuff food into their mouths at an unbelievable rate when they are under stress. A medical friend of mine used to be spooning up the last smear of custard while the rest of us were still finishing our soup. He always had digestive trouble afterwards and had to sit for half an hour to allow the pain to disappear.

2 Don't try eating while you're reading or watching television. A little mild and gentle conversation probably won't do much harm but you should concentrate as much as you can when you're eating. Only by concentrating on what you are doing will you become able to tell when your stomach is talking to you. If you listen it will talk to you, and tell you when you're eating something that is going to upset you, or eating too much.

3 Try and put small forkfuls into your mouth. Stuff huge amounts of food onto your fork and you'll end up

failing to chew your food properly. Chewing is an essential part of the digestive process and the saliva in your mouth contains enzymes which help prepare your food for the secretions produced by the stomach.

4 Try to taste each mouthful of food that you eat. That way you're far less likely to eat unnecessarily or too quickly.

5 If you are a fast eater, put down your knife and fork between mouthfuls. That will slow you down effectively.

6 Don't let other people push you into eating when you aren't hungry or when you don't want a second helping. And do be prepared to leave food on the side of your plate if you've had enough to eat.

7 When you've finished a meal have a short rest. Give your stomach time to do its job before you start chasing around again.

10. BEWARE OF FOODS THAT MAKE YOUR SYMPTOMS WORSE

Try to find out what sort of foods upset you — and then make sure that you avoid them. Different people are badly affected by different foods, so it is impossible to offer a comprehensive list of foods to avoid, but it is likely that any of the foods on the list below could exacerbate your symptoms:

All fried foods
Strong tea or coffee
Fizzy drinks
Alcohol
Fatty foods
Spicy foods
Pickles, curry, peppers, mustard
Broad beans, brussels sprouts, radishes and cucumber
Unripe fruit
Very hot or very cold foods
Coarse bread, biscuits or cereals
Nuts or dried fruit
Chocolate
Any tough food (meat for example) that can't be chewed easily

You do not necessarily have to avoid all these foods if you have digestive symptoms. But do be aware that these foods are among those that are most likely to cause problems. The important thing is to find out which foods upset you and avoid them. Do remember that *when* and *how* you eat probably affects your stomach more than *what* you eat.

11. TRY A VEGETARIAN DIET

You may find that cutting meat out of your diet helps relieve your symptoms. Here are some simple, meat free recipes designed to show you that life without meat need not be dull! I have, of course, also excluded dairy products.

SPAGHETTI NAPOLETANA

Serves 2
3oz/90g wholemeal spaghetti
1 tablespoon oil
2oz/60g mushrooms, chopped
½ green pepper, chopped
1 small carrot, chopped
1 small clove garlic, chopped
1 small onion, chopped
4oz/250g tinned tomatoes
1 tablespoon tomato puree
herbs and seasoning to taste

Cook the spaghetti in boiling water. Fry the vegetables in oil for 5 minutes. Add the tomatoes, the tomato purée and herbs and seasoning to taste. Cook for a few more minutes. Drain the spaghetti and serve with the thick vegetable sauce poured over it.

PARISIAN SALAD

Serves 2
1 orange, peeled and segmented
1 carrot, grated
½oz/15g almonds, chopped
2oz/60g celery, chopped

1 stick French bread

Break the orange segments in half, then mix the first four ingredients together. Eat with the French bread stick.

TRAVELLER'S SANDWICH

Serves 1-2
1 hard-boiled egg, finely chopped
4 tablespoons chopped cress
French mustard to taste
½ small wholemeal loaf

Mix the first three ingredients together and use as a sandwich filling.

SAVORY DUTCH CAKES

Serves 2
8oz/250g potatoes, cooked in their skins
nutmeg to taste
ground black pepper to taste
1 tablespoon soya milk
1 medium onion, finely chopped
4oz/125g cooked green vegetables

If you intend to use the oven, preheat to 180°C (350°F/Gas mark 4) and grease a baking tray. Peel the potatoes, then mash with the nutmeg and black pepper. Add the soya milk. Fry the onion without oil in a non-stick pan until tender. Mix together the potatoes, green vegetables and onion and form them into four round cakes. Bake for 10 minutes or grill under a moderate heat for 15 minutes.

GOLDEN VEGETABLE PARCELS

Serves 2
¼ pint/150ml soya milk

½ tablespoon cornflour
½ tablespoon chopped parsley
black pepper to taste
selection of leftover cooked vegetables
4oz/125g shortcrust puff pastry

Preheat the oven to 220°C (425°F/Gas mark 7) and grease a baking tray. Mix the cornflour with a little cold milk to make a smooth paste. Pour remaining milk into a saucepan, add the cornflour paste and heat slowly, and stir. Keep the milk on the heat until it has thickened, then add the parsley and season with black pepper. Add the cooked vegetables. Roll out the pastry on a floured surface and cut it into four squares. Put the vegetables into the centres of two of the pastry squares. Brush the edges of the squares with water, and then put the remaining squares on top to make 'parcels'. Pinch the edges together well to seal them. Transfer the parcels to the baking tray and bake for 25 minutes.

FRENCH BROCCOLI

Serves 2
1 tablespoon vegetable oil
2 spring onions, chopped
1 clove garlic, crushed
½ teaspoon oregano
½ teaspoon tarragon
1 tablespoon freshly chopped parsley
pinch cayenne pepper
ground black pepper to taste
12oz/350g cooked broccoli
2oz/60g breadcrumbs

Heat the oil and sauté the onions and garlic. Add the herbs and seasonings and then the broccoli. Put the mixture into a fireproof casserole. Place the breadcrumbs on top. Grill until the top appears well browned.

HOT DEVILLED EGGS

Serves 2

2 hard-boiled eggs
1 tablespoon soya yoghurt
ground black pepper to taste
pinch of dry mustard powder
paprika to taste

Shell the eggs and cut in half lengthways. Carefully remove the yolks with a sharp knife and put to one side for use in another dish, or as a sandwich filling. Add the pepper and mustard to the yoghurt and mix until smooth. Spoon the mixture into egg white hollows and sprinkle lightly with paprika.

MILANESE PEPPERS

Serves 2

1 large red or green pepper
1 tablespoon vegetable oil
1 large onion, chopped
1 clove garlic, crushed
2 tablespoons red wine
1 tablespoon tomato purée
1 tablespoon mixed chopped rosemary, oregano,
    parsley and mint
4 tablespoons vegetable stock
4oz/125g pasta shapes, uncooked
1½ oz/40g breadcrumbs
1 egg white

Preheat the oven to 180°C (350°F/Gas mark 4) and grease a baking dish. Boil the pepper in water for 1 minute. Then cool it under running water, halve and remove the seeds. Heat the oil and sauté the onion and garlic. Add the wine, tomato purée, herbs and stock. Simmer for 10 minutes. Place the pasta shapes in a large bowl. Add the bread-crumbs and egg white, mix well, then add the cooked onion and herbs. Spoon the mixture into the pepper halves and place on a baking dish. Put the entire baking dish into a shallow tray containing a little water. Cover, and bake for 35 minutes.

OAT BRAN MUFFINS

Makes about 12 American-style muffins (small cakes, not muffins for toasting)
12oz/350g oat bran
1½oz/40g mixed dried fruit
      (raisins, sultanas, currants, chopped dates, etc.)
1 tablespoon baking powder
1½oz/40g chopped, mixed nuts
2oz/60g sugar or equivalent artificial sweetener
8 fl.oz/250ml soya milk
2 tablespoons vegetable oil
2 egg whites

Preheat the oven to 220°C (425°F/Gas mark 7) and grease a 12-hole deep patty tin. Mix the oat bran, dried fruit, baking powder and nuts, then add the sugar. Mix the milk, oil and egg whites together and add to the oat bran mixture. Mix thoroughly and spoon the mixture evenly into the patty tins. Bake for 15-20 minutes or until the muffins are firm to press.

NUT BISCUITS

Makes about 10 biscuits
rice paper

2 egg whites
4oz/125g ground mixed nuts
3oz/90g sugar
2 tablespoons ground brown rice

Preheat the oven to 180°C (350°F/Gas mark 4). Grease a baking tray and line it with rice paper. Whisk the egg whites until stiff. Add the nuts and sugar, then stir in the rice. Place dollops of the mixture (allow them space to expand during baking) on the rice paper, and cook for 20–25 minutes. Serve biscuits each with their square of rice paper.

Natural muesli mix

Serves 2
2 tablespoons oats
½ tablespoon sesame seeds
½ tablespoon sunflower seeds
1 apple, sliced
1 banana, sliced
2 tablespoons mixed raisins, sultanas and currants

Mix all the ingredients together well and serve with soya milk or plain soya yoghurt.

Fruity yoghurt

Serves 2
½ pint/300ml soya yoghurt
1 apple, diced
1 orange, peeled and segmented
1 small bunch seedless grapes
¼ small melon, diced
1 banana, sliced

Mix all the ingredients together in a large bowl. Serve chilled.

VEGETABLE HOTPOT

Serves 2
1 tablespoon vegetable oil
1 medium onion, chopped
1 small turnip, sliced
1 large carrot, sliced
1 medium potato, sliced
4 sprouts, sliced
1 pint/600ml water
1 tablespoon soya sauce
1 tablespoon chopped fresh parsley

In a heavy saucepan fry the onion in the oil. Add the rest of the vegetables and half the water. Bring to the boil, them simmer covered for 20 minutes. Add the remaining water and the soya sauce. Just before serving, add the parsley.

ROYAL SALAD

Serves 2
1 cos lettuce
2 carrots
2 tomatoes
4 radishes
2oz/60g mushrooms
4 spring onions
½ small green pepper
1 apple
2 tablespoons vegetable oil
1 tablespoon cider vinegar
2oz/60g walnut pieces
1oz/30g roasted peanuts
1oz/30g raisins

Shred the lettuce. Grate and chop the vegetables and slice the apple. Combine the oil and vinegar to make a dressing and mix well with the salad. Finally, add the nuts and raisins.

WELSH MUSHROOMS

Serves 2
½ onion, finely chopped
1 clove garlic, finely chopped
1 tablespoon vegetable oil
8oz/250g mushrooms, chopped
dash of soya sauce
2 slices wholemeal toast

Sauté the onion and garlic in the oil. Add the mushrooms to the pan and cook gently. Stir in the soya sauce. Serve on hot toast.

SPAGHETTI VERONA

Serves 2
oil for frying
1 onion, chopped
1 stick celery, chopped
2 tablespoons red wine
12oz/390g tin tomatoes
1 tablespoon tomato purée
1 teaspoon dried mixed Italian herbs
¼ pint/150ml vegetable stock
6oz/175g wholewheat spaghetti

Heat the oil in a frying pan and add the onion and the celery. Add the wine and bring to the boil. Simmer for a few minutes and add the tomatoes, tomato purée and seasoning. Pour in the stock and simmer for 30 minutes. Cook the spaghetti according to the instructions on the packet, and serve immediately with the hot sauce poured over it.

PORTUGUESE HOTPOT

Serves 2
1 large potato
1 turnip
1 carrot
1 parsnip
1 onion
4oz/125g French beans
1 clove garlic
¼ pint/150ml vegetable stock
1 teaspoon lemon juice
4 tomatoes, quartered

Coarsely chop all the vegetables (except the tomatoes) and steam them. Add the vegetable stock and lemon juice. Mix well and continue to cook over a low heat. When the vegetables are just about ready, add the chopped tomatoes. Cook until vegetables ready and tomatoes warmed through.

RUSSIAN CHILLI

Serves 2
½ large onion, chopped
1 tablespoon vegetable oil
4oz/125g burghul (or bulgur) wheat
1 large tin tomatoes
1 tablespoon tomato purée
1 teaspoon chilli powder
ground black pepper to taste
½ large tin red kidney beans or 1 small tin

Sauté the onion in the oil. Add the remaining ingredients except the kidney beans and simmer until the wheat is cooked but still firm. Cook the kidney beans separately and then add.

PILOT'S PIE

Serves 2
1 tablespoon vegetable oil
3oz/90g onion, chopped
3oz/90g carrot, grated
½ teaspoon dried thyme
½ tablespoon wholemeal flour
½ teaspoon yeast extract
4oz/125g shortcrust pastry (made with polyunsaturated spread)

Preheat the oven to 190°C (375°F/Gas mark 5) and grease a baking dish. Heat the oil and sauté the onion, then add the carrot and thyme and cook gently for 10 minutes. Stir in the flour and yeast extract. Leave to cool. Roll out the pastry and line the dish with half the pastry and pile the filling into the centre. Put the remaining pastry on top and seal the edges. Make two or three small slits in the top of the pie and bake for 30 minutes.

GREEK TOMATOES

Serves 2
1 courgette
1 small aubergine
1 tablespoon vegetable oil
1 medium onion, chopped
1 clove garlic, finely chopped
1 small pepper, seeded and chopped
12oz/390g tin tomatoes
black pepper to taste

Slice the courgette and the aubergine. Leave to drain for 30 minutes. Rinse well and squeeze out any excess moisture. Heat the oil in a frying pan. Add the onion and garlic, and fry. Then add all the vegetables except the tomatoes and sauté for a few minutes. Add the tomatoes and season with black pepper. Cover and simmer for 30 minutes.

WINTER SOUP

Serves 2
1 large carrot
1 large onion
2 sticks celery
half small turnip
2 medium sized potatoes
½ pint/300ml vegetable stock
6 sprigs parsley
grated nutmeg to taste
grated black pepper to taste

Chop all the vegetables and put them into a large saucepan. Add the stock and simmer for 1 hour. Just before the end of the cooking time add the parsley. Season with the grated nutmeg and black pepper.

JAMAICAN RICE

Serves 2
1 tablespoon vegetable oil
half large onion, sliced
half red apple, sliced
pinch of curry powder
½ pint/300ml water
4oz/125g brown rice
1 teaspoonful black treacle
1 small banana, sliced
1 tablespoonful desiccated coconut

Heat the oil and sauté the onion and apple. Add the curry powder and water. Bring to the boil. Add the rice and treacle and cook until the water is absorbed and the rice is tender. Drain and add the banana. Sprinkle the coconut on top and heat through for a moment. Then serve.

BANANA SPECIAL

Serves 2
2 bananas
1 small orange, juiced
1oz/30g sugar
1oz/15g polyunsaturated low-fat spread

Preheat the oven to 180°C (350°F/Gas mark 4), and grease an ovenproof dish. Peel the bananas, cut them in half lengthways and place them in the dish. Pour the orange juice over the bananas and sprinkle the sugar on top. Place the low-fat spread on top of the bananas and cook for 15 minutes.

SPICY RED PEAR

Serves 1
1 large pear
4 tablespoons red wine
ground or whole spices – ginger, cinnamon and cloves

Peel the pear, leaving it whole with the stalk on. Simmer in the red wine with the spices until cooked. Serve hot.

FRUIT PUNCH

Makes about 1 pint/600ml
1 pint/600ml natural (unsweetened) pineapple juice
1 banana, sliced
1 apple, chopped
1oz/30g sesame seeds
1oz/30g sunflower seeds
1oz/30g raisins
1oz/30g currants

Put all the ingredients in a blender and liquidise. Keep in the refrigerator and serve chilled.

Step 2
CONTROL THE STRESS IN YOUR LIFE

Since I first wrote about stress in my book *Stress Control* nearly 20 years ago, most other doctors have slowly come to agree with my contention that stress plays a vital part in the development of 90% of all illnesses.

Today it is widely recognised that we are all exposed to stress. Stress is all around us. It is unavoidable. We all respond to it in different ways. Some people never seem to suffer from stress related illnesses at all while others seem exceptionally fragile and susceptible. It isn't the amount of stress that you are under that decides whether or not you develop irritable bowel syndrome — and whether or not your symptoms flare up and get worse — but the way that you respond to the stress in your life. The following pages of this book are designed to help you learn how to reduce your exposure to stress and how to increase your ability to resist stress. You will not need to follow all the advice on these pages but selecting the advice which you consider most appropriate will, I believe, help you to bring the symptoms of your irritable bowel syndrome under control.

1. HOW HEALTHY IS YOUR MIND?

This self screening questionnaire is designed to help you discover any weak points in your personality before serious problems develop. Answer the questions carefully — and honestly — and find out if you need to change the way you live in order to strengthen your mind, reduce your susceptibility to stress and help get rid of your symptoms!

1. ARE YOU LOOKING FORWARD TO THE NEXT 12 MONTHS?

a) a lot   score AAA
b) a bit   score AA
c) not at all   score A

2. DO YOU WORRY ABOUT THINGS EVEN THOUGH YOU KNOW THAT THEY ARE UNIMPORTANT?

a) a lot   score BBB
b) a bit   score BB
c) not at all   score B

3. DO YOU FIND YOURSELF APOLOGISING TO PEOPLE?

a) a lot   score CCC
b) a bit   score CC
c) not at all   score C

4. DO YOU THINK YOU ARE A GOOD LOVER?

a) yes   score C
b) no   score CCC

5. DO YOU HAVE DREAMS AND HOPES FOR THE FUTURE?

a) no   score A
b) yes, a few   score AA
c) yes, a lot   score AAA

6. DO YOU TELL THOSE WHOM YOU LOVE HOW YOU FEEL?

a) a lot   score DDD
b) a bit   score DD
c) not at all   score D

7. IN A RESTAURANT THE SERVICE IS POOR. WOULD YOU STILL LEAVE A TIP?

a) yes   score E
b) no   score EEE

8. ARE YOU EASILY INTIMIDATED BY OTHER PEOPLE — PARTICULARLY PEOPLE IN UNIFORM?

a) yes   score E
b) no   score EEE

9. DO YOU FEEL EMBARRASSED OR ASHAMED OF YOURSELF?

a) a lot   score CCC
b) a bit   score CC
c) not at all   score C

10. DO YOU GET UP IN THE MORNING LOOKING FORWARD TO THE DAY AHEAD?

a) always   score AAA
b) occasionally   score AA
c) never   score A

11. DO YOU FEEL EMBARRASSED BY PUBLIC DISPLAYS OF AFFECTION?

a) a lot   score D
b) a bit   score DD
c) not at all   score DDD

12. DO YOU FIND IT DIFFICULT TO RELAX?

a) a lot   score BBB
b) a bit   score BB
c) not at all   score B

13. HOW OFTEN DO YOU GET UPSET WHEN THINGS BREAK DOWN?

a) a lot   score BBB
b) a bit   score BB
c) not at all   score B

14. DO YOU KEEP YOUR FEELINGS TO YOURSELF?

a) always   score D
b) sometimes   score DD
c) never   score DDD

Now add up the number of As, Bs, Cs, Ds and Es that you've scored.

If you scored less than 5 "A"s

You're too much of a pessimist. The only advantage of being a pessimist is that because you expect little you're rarely disappointed. But pessimism can easily lead to anger, frustration, confusion and serious depression. Every time anything goes wrong your attitude will ensure that gloom will deepen. Try to establish a more positive approach to life. Try to make plans for the future that excite you. Begin new projects and make new friends with high hopes. A cautious, negative approach is bad for your mental and physical health.

If you scored more than 5 "B"s

You need to learn to relax. You're a worrier and worry can do your mind — and your body — enormous damage. Try to spend at least half a day a week doing something that you find truly relaxing. Many people find that taking up a new hobby is particularly relaxing.

If you scored more than 5 "C"s

You need more self confidence. The chances are that although you know what your weaknesses are you don't know what your strengths are. Sit down with a piece of paper and write down all the good things you can say about yourself. For example, which of these adjectives describe you: honest, generous, thoughtful, hard working, punctual, careful, moral, kind, ambitious, creative?

If you scored less than 5 "D"s

Holding in your emotions can damage your mental and physical health. Stored up inside you sadness and anger can cause a considerable amount of damage. Try to share your feelings with other people. Talk to friends when you feel sad, happy or upset. Don't be afraid to show how you feel — with a kiss or a hug. Don't be afraid to cry if you feel like crying. And remember that saying "I love you" to the people you love can help them as well as you.

If you scored less than 3 "E"s

You need to stand up for yourself more. Your life is being run by other people — and that can cause anger and frustration. Learn to stand your ground and stick up for yourself. You don't have to be rude — just be honest. You'll gain the self respect of others. If you don't want to do something say so — as simply and as honestly as possible. If you feel you ought to complain then do so. The more you do it the easier it will become. You'll be surprised to find that people soon treat you with more consideration.

2. STAND UP FOR YOURSELF

How will you spend the coming weekend? How much time will you spend doing things that you really want to do? And how much time will you spend doing things that you aren't looking forward to — but that other people want you to do?

I'd like you to make two lists of how you're likely to spend your time. On the first list put the things you're looking forward to — the things you'll enjoy. On the second list put the things that you feel you ought to do, the things you think other people expect you to do and the things you're not looking forward to at all. Put down everything: meals, TV programmes, visitors, parties, trips to the pub, chores.

Now see which list is longer.

If your second list is the longer then you need to stand up for yourself more. The chances are that you get pushed around a lot by just about everyone you know — friends, relatives and employers especially. You probably do errands for people who could perfectly well do their own errands. You're probably the sort of person who gets lumbered with looking after the children while everyone else goes off to a party. You work overtime and don't get paid for it. You get the boring jobs when you're on a committee. And you never dream of complaining when you get rotten service in shops and restaurants.

You're too shy, too soft hearted and too nice to complain or say 'no'. You don't stick up for yourself. And the chances are that your health is suffering. Your IBS is probably a result of the fact that you get pushed around too much.

I'm not suggesting that you try to turn yourself into a selfish bully. But you do need to stand up for yourself a little more.

Learning how to assert yourself — and stick up for yourself — isn't difficult.

Here's my advice:

1 *Always try to be honest*

If you don't want to do something, say so. If you don't tell people you're unhappy about something they won't know! If you try to offer explanations or excuses then you'll probably end up trapping yourself. So, for example, if you're invited to a meeting and you don't want to go don't lie and say that you're busy that day. If you do you'll be trapped if the date of the meeting is changed.

2 *Remember that you're an individual and you have rights*

Of course you should try to help people who are less fortunate than you — particularly the old, the young and the disabled. But don't let yourself be suckered into looking after people who can look after themselves. Thousands of mothers and fathers spend their days acting as slaves for teenagers who could (and should) do more for themselves. You have a right to some fun in your life.

3 *Stop apologising unnecessarily*

If you're always saying sorry and feeling guilty then people will for ever be taking advantage of you. Only say 'sorry' when you really mean it.

3. BUILD UP YOUR SELF CONFIDENCE

Are you riddled with self doubt? Do you wish you had more self assurance? Would you like to be able to walk into a room feeling confident?

The tips which follow are designed to help you build up your self confidence! The more you can build up your confidence the less susceptible you will be to guilt, to destructive feelings of inadequacy and to excessive self criticism. You will also be stronger when you are confronted by people who want you to do things that you don't really want to do. And by building up your self confidence you will be much better equipped to deal with stress. Your susceptibility to IBS will diminish and I suspect that you will suffer far fewer symptoms.

You must replace negative, damaging feelings of failure, incompetence and unworthiness with positive feelings of success.

1 Begin by writing an advertisement extolling your virtues and listing all your good points. Look down this list and tick the words which you honestly feel apply to you:

☐ honest
☐ truthful
☐ romantic
☐ honourable
☐ punctilious
☐ scrupulous
☐ attentive

- [ ] faithful
- [ ] decent
- [ ] moral
- [ ] conscientious
- [ ] respectable
- [ ] law-abiding
- [ ] chivalrous
- [ ] unselfish
- [ ] impeccable
- [ ] obedient
- [ ] benevolent
- [ ] kind
- [ ] careful
- [ ] creative
- [ ] ambitious
- [ ] hard-working
- [ ] brave
- [ ] witty
- [ ] wise
- [ ] intelligent
- [ ] polite
- [ ] punctual
- [ ] thoughtful
- [ ] fastidious
- [ ] agreeable
- [ ] welcoming
- [ ] skilful

2   Remember that there is nothing wrong in saying: 'I was wrong. I am sorry'. If you accept challenges, take risks and live your life to the full then sometimes you will fail. Although making a mistake is a weakness, admitting that you have made a mistake is a sign of strength and courage. Apologising for your mistakes is a sign of maturity and learning from your mistakes is a sign of true wisdom. People who never make mistakes never take chances and people who never take chances have a life full of missed opportunities and permanent regrets.

3   It may sound strange but I think you should try to be more selfish. People who have a low self esteem and who suffer a lot from guilt tend to be selfless — and tend to spend much of their lives worrying about and thinking about other people. If you are a guilt sufferer you probably need to spend more time thinking about what *you* want.

4   On the days when you feel that your life is a failure and you wish that you had more to be proud of, make a list of all the things in your life that are really important to you: partner, friends, health, children, integrity, interests, accomplishments, work, skills, knowledge and memories. You will probably be surprised to find how many things there are that you can be proud about!

5   When anxieties about the future become most worrying ask yourself what is the worst that can happen. You will probably be surprised to find that the 'worst' may not be as bad as you thought it was going to be. The 'bottom line' often isn't as daunting as you think it will be.

4. EXERCISE YOUR MIND

Every doctor in the world agrees that some *physical* exercise is an essential part of a healthy life. And there are hundreds of exercise programmes and videos designed to show you how to exercise safely and effectively. But most people ignore their *minds* — they don't give them any useful exercise at all. And yet the right mental exercise can work wonders — and help you control your IBS.

In recent years researchers all around the world have shown that if you replace unhappy feelings and miserable memories with good feelings and good memories you can make yourself feel much better. By focusing on good memories and happy thoughts you can:

- improve your physical and mental strength
- improve your immunity to infections and other diseases
- conquer sleeplessness
- achieve your ambitions and become more successful in just about every area of your life

Begin by finding yourself a notebook and a pencil — and a quiet spot. Then think back and decide which are the seven happiest days you've ever spent — the seven happiest days of your life.

Go right back to your childhood. Think really hard.

Think of the days which have made you feel really good: a holiday, a day out, a special birthday, a Christmas celebration, an exam success, meeting someone you love, a wedding day, moving into a new home, a reunion, the birth of a child.

The more you think the more really good days you'll remember.

Make a list of your favourite seven — that's now your new all-time favourite week.

When you think of the good days from your past try to relive them.

Try to experience once again the sounds and smells of each of your seven favourite days. Close your eyes and try to see those days: the weather, the people, the buildings, everything.

Concentrate hard until you begin to feel as good as you did on those very special days in your life.

Try to remember the way you felt: the joy, the warmth, the happiness.

The really strange thing about this exercise is that the best memories from your past can make the present seem much better too.

Try thinking through your favourite week first thing in the morning and last thing at night.

Do it again when you're feeling glum or downcast — or when things seem to be going badly wrong.

You'll be astonished to see just how these uplifting memories can improve life for you.

And always remember that however bad today may seem to be, there is always a chance that tomorrow may win a place in your all-time favourite week!

5. RELAX YOUR BODY

If you're going to learn how to relax properly then you need twenty minutes a day when you won't be disturbed. That's all.

If you join my easy-to-follow relaxation class, then in just two weeks you'll be able to relax so well that you'll be able to get rid of your tension wherever you are and whatever you are doing.

Tension tightens your muscles because your body is responding to the stress you're under. Your body assumes that because you feel anxious you are in danger. It assumes that you are physically threatened and it tenses your muscles so that you will be better able to fight or run away.

But tensed muscles lead to a worsening of your irritable bowel syndrome symptoms.

If you are going to learn how to conquer the stress in your life — and relax effectively — you *must* plan your relaxation programme carefully.

- If you've got children get someone else to look after them.
- If you've got a telephone take it off the hook.
- Go into a room where you can be quiet and alone.
- Close the curtains.
- Turn off the lights.
- Lie or sit down somewhere really comfortable.

  Now, follow my 20 point relaxation plan.

1   Clench your right hand as tightly as you can, making a fist with your fingers. Count up to ten while you hold

your fingers tight and tense. If you now gradually let your fingers unfold you will feel your muscles slowly relaxing.

2 Bend your right arm and try to make your left biceps muscle stand out. Again, count up to ten. Then lay your arm down loosely by your side.

3 Relax your left hand in the same way that you relaxed your right hand.

4 Relax your right arm, then lay it down by your side and forget about it.

5 Curl the toes in your right foot as tightly as you can. Count up to ten. Then relax those muscles.

6 Move your right foot so that your toes are pointing up towards your knee. Count up to ten. You should feel the muscles in your calf becoming tighter. Then relax.

7 Try to push your right foot away from you. You should feel the muscles in your right thigh tightening up. Count up to ten. Then relax.

8 Relax your left foot.

9 Relax your left lower leg.

10 Relax your left thigh.

11 Tighten up the muscles in your bottom so that your whole body lifts up an inch or so. Count up to ten. Then relax.

12 Try to pull your abdominal muscles in towards your spine. Count up to ten. Then relax.

13 Take a big breath in. Count up to ten. Then relax.

14 Keep your head still and try to touch your ears with your shoulders. It will probably be impossible but try anyway. Count to ten. Then relax.

15 Stretch your neck as far away from your chest as you

can. Count to ten. Then deliberately relax those muscles too. Move your head around in all directions to make sure that your neck muscles are free and easy.

16 Stretch the muscles of your back. Try to make yourself as tall as you can. Count to ten. Then relax.

17 Move your eyebrows as high as you can. Hold them high up while you count up to ten. Then relax.

18 Screw up your eyes very tightly. Pretend that someone is trying to force them open. Count to ten then, keeping your eyes closed, relax those muscles too.

19 Push your tongue out as far as it will go. Count to ten. Then relax.

20 Smile as wide as you possibly can. Count to ten. Then relax.

All this should have taken you slightly less than ten minutes. And every muscle in your body should now be thoroughly relaxed.

6. RELAX YOUR MIND

Try to imagine that you are lying on a warm, sunny beach.

It is *your* personal, private beach. There is no one else there. And no one else will ever be allowed onto it.

Then use all your senses to help soothe away all your anxieties and all your everyday pressures.

- FEEL the sun on your face and body.
- LISTEN to the sound of the sea in the distance and the seagulls circling high overhead.
- SMELL the salt sea air.

The more you can convince yourself that you are lying, relaxed and calm, on a warm, sunny beach the more effectively you will be able to escape from your daily worries.

If you practise this simple exercise *every day* for a *fortnight,* you will find that you will gradually get more and more skilled at relaxing your body and your mind.

Soon, you should be able to relax yourself within a minute. And, most important of all, you will be able to relax wherever you are and whatever you are doing.

Within a fortnight you should be able to relax both your body and your mind: in a queue in your local shop, while waiting for a bus or train or while doing the washing up. All you will have to do is imagine that you are lying on your own, personal, warm, sunny beach.

7. USE YOUR POSITIVE EMOTIONS

You can't escape from your emotions — they rule your life.

Your emotions decide whether or not you're going to be happy. They determine the sort of personality you have. And decide how successful you become.

Most important of all, however, your emotions have a powerful effect on your health. It is your emotions which often decide whether or not your IBS is going to flare up.

In this section of the book I'm going to deal with positive emotions. I'll deal with negative emotions in the next section.

1. LAUGHTER

When you laugh your lungs are exercised and your heart is given excellent 'tuning up' exercise. More importantly, special healing hormones are released inside your body! After a good laugh your blood pressure will be lower, your breathing will be easier and you will sleep better.

You'll find work easier. And your relationships with friends and strangers will be improved.

Try it: next time you're feeling miserable try putting a really cheerful smile on your face. You'll find it difficult to stay quite so sad. Try making your eyes sparkle with laughter and you'll notice the effect even more. Smile at the people you meet and you'll get on with them better. People will like you better if you smile!

Keep a few favourite 'funny' videos around for when you're feeling low. (But take care: researchers have shown that you'll benefit more by watching simple, uncomplicated 'clown' type humour than by watching cruel, satirical or political comedy.)

2. LOVE

When I was a newly qualified junior hospital doctor a stunningly attractive woman in her early twenties was brought onto the ward where I was working. She had meningitis and the infection seemed to be winning. It looked as though she was going to die. She had been married for six months and her husband would not leave her side. He held her hand, stroked her cheek and talked to her. For hour after hour he told her that he loved her. He wiped away his tears with her hand. He kissed her gently on the lips and he murmured her name over and over again.

He would not let her go.

Slowly he hauled her back to life. Little by little she regained her strength. To this day I firmly believe that it was his love — not our drugs — that saved her life.

More recently researchers around the world have produced evidence showing that the power of love does have remarkable healing potential.

- Patients with cancer stand a better chance of surviving if they are shown love and affection while they fight their disease.

- Insurance companies in the USA have shown that if a wife kisses her husband goodbye when he goes off to work every morning he will be less likely to have a car accident — and he'll live about 5 years longer than the man who goes to work without a kiss.

- Babies and children who get lots of love grow up healthier than children who are deprived of affection.

3. HOPE

If your life has hope, purpose and meaning you will be happier and healthier than people whose lives don't have hope or purpose!

One patient of mine won a small fortune on the pools.

Up until his big win he had worked hard at his job as a gardener — it was a job which he thoroughly enjoyed.

When he had his big win he gave up work. He said he was going to enjoy life! But within six months he had become ill and frail. He looked ten years older. He had lost the purpose in his life. He had nothing to look forward to.

He only recovered his health when he started work again.

'Looking forward to seeing seeds come up gives me a thrill,' he told me. 'It makes life worth living.'

We all need a purpose in our lives. We need something to hope for, something to fight for and something to look forward to. Without purpose our lives become hollow and unrewarding. And our health suffers. If your life lacks hope and purpose try to recall the goals and ambitions you had when you were teenager. Then see which of them you can revive.

Whatever your age your life needs purpose and direction as it needs food and oxygen. You need to be stretched and you need to take chances.

4. OPTIMISM

Not all people can be clearly defined as 'optimists' or 'pessimists' but most people are mainly one or the other.

Pessimists always tend to look on the black side. And suffer from terrible health. Most IBS sufferers will admit that they worry about many things which they don't really need to worry about. They worry because they constantly — and unjustifiably — fear the worst.

Optimists put failures behind them, do their best to look on the bright side — and generally have much better health than pessimists.

8. CONTROL YOUR NEGATIVE EMOTIONS

1. ANGER

Whatever causes it, anger can damage your physical and your mental health. It can 'create' the irritable bowel syndrome — and then make symptoms worse.

Problems usually arise when anger is suppressed. That's when it causes high blood pressure, heart attacks, strokes — and IBS.

Hold your anger in and you'll be more likely to suffer from IBS than if you let it out in a harmless way.

Everyone gets angry from time to time. Anger is produced by indifference, impatience and thoughtlessness in others.

To avoid the damage that anger can do you must learn to cope with it. If you feel yourself getting angry try to decide if your anger is justified. If it is then say something. If it isn't then try to walk away from the cause of your anger. Don't be afraid to complain or speak out if you feel strongly about some injustice. You may also be able to get rid of excess anger with physical activity. Try going for a walk if you are angry. You may find it helps.

2. FEAR

Fear is a way of life these days.

We are encouraged to worry by just about everyone. We worry about money, war and the environment. We worry about the ozone layer, inner city violence and pollution. Most of all we worry about our health. 'Scare' stories (many of them unnecessary) are turning us into a nation of hypochondriacs.

Too often our fears about our health actually make us ill! People who suffer from IBS tend to be sensitive and susceptible. Their sensitivity and susceptibility mean that they are easily frightened.

- Try to identify, recognise and face your fears. Decide precisely what worries you. Never forget that the spectre in the dark is more dangerous then the fear you can examine.

- Whatever it is that frightens you — learn as much as you can about it. If you're frightened of spiders, get a book on spiders out of the library. Fears are often based on myths and superstitions and half-heard facts. The truth often demolishes fears.

- If you have a specific fear about your health then get professional advice. If, for example, you fear that your IBS symptoms may suggest some more serious under-lying problem, you should consult your doctor instead of simply worrying.

- Try to put your fear into perspective. We often worry far too much about things that are never likely to happen. Put into perspective some of your most damaging fears will probably disappear.

- Don't spend too much time watching worrying television programmes. And don't spend too much time reading alarming and worrying news in the newspapers.

3. BOREDOM

Inactivity and boredom, and not having enough to do or enough responsibility, can damage your health just as much as too much pressure. Boredom is dangerous. It can cause heart disease, skin trouble and depression as well as IBS.

Here are some of the ways in which you can tackle boredom:

- Take up a hobby or pastime that you find rewarding and exciting. Do something that you can take pride in.

- Consider establishing a small business of your own. Many small businesses need very little capital. And you may be entitled to a grant.

- When stuck with boring tasks escape into fantasy daydreams.

4. SADNESS

Sadness is our natural way of reacting to problems, pressures and stresses. And the natural way of showing that we are sad is by crying. When we are young and unhappy we cry quite naturally to make it clear to our parents — and to everyone around us — that we need attention, sympathy and love.

As we grow older we find that shedding tears is a quick way to tell the people who love us that we need their affection.

Recently scientists have managed to show that shedding tears provides us with a genuine, physical release.

Tears shed for emotional reasons have a higher protein content than tears shed because of physical irritations. Crying helps the body get rid of harmful physical wastes. If you don't cry when you're sad you're more likely to end up depressed.

Many people wrongly regard crying as a sign of weakness — and even of emotional instability. Boys and men in particular are encouraged to bottle up their feelings. But when people don't cry they suffer badly. If you suppress your tears you store your sadness inside you; your body retains unwanted chemical wastes and you deny yourself a powerful therapy. Crying is an excellent way of dealing with sadness; after crying most people feel calm and rested in a strange sort of way.

5. GUILT

Guilt is one of the most damaging of all human emotions. It's hard to distinguish from what most of us call 'conscience'.

We feel guilty when we've done wrong or when we've failed to do something that we know we should have done. We then torture ourselves with recriminations.

Ironically, much of our guilt is created within us by the people we love!

First, there is the guilt found in personal relationships. Sometimes this is produced deliberately — as when a mum says 'You wouldn't do that if you loved me' (and the child is made to feel guilty). Sometimes the guilt is produced more subtly. As, when one person says to another: 'Don't you worry about me — I'll be all right' (making the person worry — and feel guilty!).

Second, there is the guilt that results from the teachings of those around us. Religious teachings often make us guilty whatever we do! Many people feel guilty if they enjoy themselves, have sex or lie in bed on Sunday mornings!

Guilt is a major cause of stress. It makes us overwork. It causes all the diseases related to stress.

To counteract guilt try to build up your self confidence. Think of your virtues and your value and your strengths. The more you're aware of the way guilt can rule your life the stronger and more resistant to it you'll become.

9. THE VALUE OF TOUCHING

The chances are that you touch the people you love far too little. And you probably need to give out more cuddles too.

Touching — and being touched — is good for everyone. If small children aren't touched often they quickly become seriously depressed. They may stop eating and simply fade away. It's not unknown for a child to die of love starvation. Even when things don't get that bad children often suffer lasting damage if they aren't touched and cuddled frequently. Children who are deprived of physical love as children often grow up to be promiscuous — unable to settle down with one partner as they are driven on in an endless search for more and more love.

It isn't only children who suffer if they're deprived of hugs and cuddles. Without regular signs of physical affection we all become brittle, unstable and more susceptible to stress and pressure.

Ask yourself how many times you've hugged the people who are closest to you in the last 24 hours. And ask yourself how often you've touched the people you love.

If your parents didn't hug or cuddle you very often you may find it difficult to let yourself go. You may have even been encouraged to believe that hugging, cuddling and touching are embarrassing or too 'showy'. Boys are often told off for wanting a hug. 'You're too old for that sort of thing,' Father will say because he feels uncomfortable at the prospect of close physical contact.

If you think that you need to touch — and be touched — more often, make today the day you start.

● When you greet a loved one — even if it's only after a

few hours' parting — put an arm around them. You don't have to start with a full blooded hug if that makes you feel embarrassed. Build up to a hug slowly!

- When you're leaving someone — again if it's only for a few hours — touch them on the arm or shoulder. Try a peck on the cheek if you're shy about a full mouth to mouth kiss. Again, build up to a proper cuddle.

- Don't let children fool you when they wriggle away if you're trying to hug them. All children like to receive physical signs of affection (though they may be embarrassed about it in public if other children's parents don't show any signs of affection). Wait until you're somewhere private to show how you feel.

- When you kiss someone 'hello' or 'goodbye' don't be content with a distant peck on the cheek. Put your arms around them, give them a big hug.

- When you greet close friends get into the habit of touching them — maybe clasping their hands or forearm, or perhaps putting an arm around them.

Hugging, touching and kissing aren't just for lovers. If you regularly hug, touch and kiss all the people who matter to you then you'll feel better — and so will they!

10. HOW TO DEAL WITH THE 'MISERIES'

IBS sufferers often feel fed up or miserable for no very good reason. If you fall into this category, and your doctor has told you that there is nothing he can do for you, I've devised a 15 point plan to help you put a smile on your face and a spring in your step. Please note, however, that as with the rest of this book this section is not intended to replace professional medical advice from an advisor whom you trust. It is particularly important that you get advice from your doctor if you feel depressed or anxious.

1 Start taking more exercise. Join a gym. Visit the local swimming pool. Make an effort to *do* something physical. Its too easy to slump down in front of the TV set. Your body needs regular work-outs. Without exercise you'll become stale, flaccid and vulnerable to germs.

2 If you normally go to bed at the same time every evening try staying up late at night — watch a movie, go out to a party or just invite friends round. Surprising though it may sound going without sleep occasionally can banish a depression quickly.

3 Work out how many of your waking hours you spend doing things you want to do; and how many you spend doing things that other people want you to do. If you spend more than 50% of your time doing things for other people make an effort to be more selfish. Make more time for yourself.

4 If your house is dimly lit buy bigger light bulbs. Living in half dark rooms can be depressing. Put a 150 watt bulb in place of a 100 watt bulb and you're unlikely to

notice much difference in your electricity bill but you may well feel more cheerful.

5 Eat less. Most of us eat far too much — especially in winter when rolls of fat are covered up by layers of thick clothes. Too much food will make you lethargic and tired. When you put food on your plate ask yourself if you really *need* that much. If not, take less.

6 Make plans so that you have things to look forward to every week. It doesn't have to be anything complicated or expensive. Plan to meet a friend, go for a walk, see a movie. And don't let yourself pull out at the last minute because you want to slump down in front of the television.

7 Drink lots of fresh water and fruit juices. If you drink lots of tea or coffee drink it fairly weak. Eat lots of fresh fruit and vegetables — your body needs the vitamins.

8 Make a real effort to look after your appearance — even if the weather is lousy and you have nowhere to go. Wearing bright, cheerful clothes — and looking good — will improve the way you feel. Try to avoid clothes in dark colours.

9 Frustration, tension, anger and worry all lead to stiff, uncomfortable muscles. The result is usually headaches and other pains. Try massaging your temples with your finger tips every evening. In fact, you'll feel fresher if you gently massage the whole of your face with your finger tips.

10 Wear the underwear you keep for very special occasions — the flimsiest, sexiest and most outrageous things you've got. It may not do much towards keeping you warm but it'll make you feel good when you're standing in the bus queue.

11 Send silly postcards to your five best friends — for no reason at all. It'll make you feel better and it'll make them feel good too.

12 If you're feeling physically exhausted as well as mentally fed up, spend twenty minutes in a warm bath with a good book or magazine.

13 Go through the TV listings magazines and pick out programmes that you know you'll enjoy. The joy of anticipation is never disappointing.

14 Try this simple exercise to calm your entire body: take a deep breath; suck in your tummy muscles to make your tummy as hard as it will go; count to five; let your muscles go limp; empty the air out of your lungs. Repeat this several times until you feel thoroughly relaxed.

15 Choose a new hobby — something that you've always wanted to try. Enrol in evening classes, borrow a book from the library or join a correspondence course. A new hobby will put passion and excitement back into your life.

11. USE EXERCISE TO COMBAT STRESS

WARNING

1. DO NOT START AN EXERCISE PROGRAMME UNTIL YOU HAVE CHECKED WITH YOUR DOCTOR THAT THE PROGRAMME IS SUITABLE FOR YOU. MAKE SURE THAT YOU TELL HIM ABOUT ANY TREATMENT YOU ARE ALREADY RECEIVING AND ABOUT ANY SYMPTOMS FROM WHICH YOU SUFFER.

2. YOU MUST STOP EXERCISING IF YOU FEEL FAINT, DIZZY, BREATHLESS OR NAUSEATED OR IF YOU NOTICE ANY PAIN OR IF YOU FEEL UNWELL IN ANY WAY. GET EXPERT HELP IMMEDI-ATELY AND DO NOT START EXERCISING AGAIN UNTIL YOU HAVE BEEN GIVEN THE 'ALL CLEAR' BY YOUR DOCTOR.

Stress, muscle tension and pain are interlinked and inex-tricable. If you are under stress your muscles will be tense. If your muscles are tense they will feel painful. The pain you get when you are under stress depends upon which muscles are tensed. If the muscles around your head are tensed, you will get a headache. If the muscles around your bowel are tensed, you will probably end up suffering from the pains and other symptoms associated with IBS.

Exercise helps to break up the muscle tension in several ways:

- When you commit yourself to exercise you deliberately put aside your daily worries and anxieties. By concen-trating on what you are doing you force the stresses in your life into the back of your mind — and both your mind and your body benefit.

- By stretching your muscles exercise helps to remove accumulated tensions. As the tension goes so the pain disappears too.

- Many of the accumulated stresses in your body are a result of frustrations and disappointments and uncommitted anger. Modern life leads us into many situations where we want to explode — but where we know that losing our temper would be inappropriate or illegal. Our body's natural response to stress (which wants us to respond physically) leads to a build up of muscle tension. The change in your muscles is designed to enable you to fight or to run away. But usually you do neither. When you exercise your body you give yourself a chance to empty your muscles of those accumulated stresses and tensions.

- Regular exercise encourages your body to produce soothing and healing hormones called endorphins — your body's own version of the opiates. These hormones will help heal your ills and make you feel better.

- A sensible, regular exercise programme that improves your general health and fitness will increase your resistance to stress and reduce your susceptibility to stress related illnesses.

- People who exercise regularly produce lower levels of a stress related hormone called epinephrine (also known as adrenalin) and experience less dramatic blood pressure and heart rate rises during ordinary types of everyday stress. As a result regular exercisers are far less likely to suffer from heart disease. At the same time, argue some experts, the production of a chemical called norepinephrine (also known as noradrenalin) increases dramatically during and after exercise and helps combat depression, increase happiness levels and tackle stress.

Despite the well known value of exercise, the chances

are high that you don't take enough of it. Too little exercise can increase your chances of developing IBS. Regular, gentle exercise can help you deal with the symptoms.

The first thing you must do is check with your doctor if you are in any doubt about your fitness to undertake an exercise programme. Everyone starting an exercise programme should get their doctor's approval before they start.

Don't just rush down to your gym and start lifting the heaviest weights you can find or pedalling the exercise bicycle as fast as it will go — you'll almost certainly make yourself ill if you do. And you could kill yourself.

Try to find a gym with a good coach, a well run aerobics class or a sports club that you can join. If you are unused to exercise a good coach is particularly vital: he or she will show you how to take your pulse *before* and *after* every exercise session. Within a few weeks you should notice that your pulse will go back to its normal rate quicker and quicker after exercising. You should also notice that your normal pulse rate gets lower as you get fitter.

One of the by-products of taking up an exercise programme is that you'll meet new friends with whom you can share the trials and tribulations of getting fit. You'll do better and get more out of your exercise programme if it is *fun* so try to choose a type of exercise that you think you'll enjoy.

Allocate time for exercise and stick to it. If you decide to exercise only when you've got a free moment you'll never do anything. You need to set aside time for a properly organised exercise programme. But it need not be much. Three sessions a week will be plenty. You should allow a full hour for each session though to start with you probably won't be able to manage that much. If you are really pushed for time you can squeeze a useful exercise programme into just three twenty minute sessions. Can there be anyone who is so busy that they can't manage one hour a week? Try to make your exercise time inviolable and give it priority over other, less vital tasks.

And do remember the most important rule for exercise: it should never hurt. Pain is your body's way of saying *stop*. If you ignore a pain — and attempt to blunder bravely through the pain barrier — you will almost certainly injure yourself.

Once you have started an exercise programme, try to continue with it. The human body was designed to be used and, like a machine, it works best when it is used regularly. If you leave a car sitting in the garage for months at a time and you don't even start the engine occasionally then you'll probably have difficulty in getting it to move when you finally need it, and you'll certainly find that it will behave sluggishly to begin with. The human body is the same. If you don't do any exercise at all then your heart will grow weak, your muscles will become flabby and your whole body will become inefficient and less capable of coping with illness or pressure. Regular exercise helps to ensure that your body becomes better able to cope with emergencies of all kinds and more capable of resisting illness and infection. A sensible, well organised, regular exercise programme will help ensure that you are less likely to suffer from dozens of different disorders — including the symptoms of IBS.

If you are not very fit you must remember that your exercise programme must start slowly and gently and then gradually build up as your fitness improves.

The words 'gentle' and 'regular' are important, by the

way. If you start an exhausting and over demanding exercise programme there is a real risk that you will injure yourself. And if you exercise only occasionally you will never become properly fit.

In order to make sure that you build up your physical fitness slowly and carefully — and without injury — you should follow these simple rules:

Rule 1

Always talk to your doctor first — and get his approval and permission for your planned exercise programme.

Rule 2

It is vitally important that before an exercise session you should make sure you loosen your joints and warm up your muscles as well as you can. If you exercise with cold muscles and stiff joints you will increase your chances of acquiring an injury. Similarly, it is important that you cool down after an exercise session. A good aerobics teacher

---

WALK YOUR WAY TO FITNESS

You don't have to get hot and sweaty to improve your fitness or to get rid of stress.

A gentle walk can provide you with enough beneficial exercise to reduce your chances of suffering from heart disease and to reduce your susceptibility to stress.

A study of golfers showed that just walking round a golf course three times a week is enough to reduce the amount of cholesterol in the blood stream and to help get rid of excess weight!

And the more you enjoy your walk, and the better you are able to forget your worries and anxieties, the more you will benefit from it.

To really benefit from your exercise walk as briskly as you can. Brisk walking protects your heart just as well as more energetic exercise such as jogging or playing tennis.

---

will always make sure that her or his class members all warm up and cool down properly.

Rule 3

If you exercise every day you will become mentally and physically tired. So try to take a rest day between exercise sessions. To get the best result from your exercise programme try to exercise three times a week. (If you are to benefit properly you should exercise at least twice a week and no more than five times a week).

Rule 4

If you are going to benefit fully an exercise session should last at least ten minutes and preferably at least twenty minutes. Do not exercise for too long until you have attained a reasonable standard of fitness.

Rule 5

Always talk to a good coach before you start exercising. Get him or her to help you with advice. And make sure that he or she knows about any illness or medical condition you may have.

12. HOW WORRYING MORE CAN HELP YOU WORRY LESS

Are you a worrier? Are you the sort of person who worries about anything and everything?

If so then you may be able to help yourself by taking your worrying more seriously — and spending more time on it!

A team of researchers in America have shown that people who allocate fixed amounts of time for worrying suffer less torment — and fewer side effects of stress — than people who always try to push their worries into the background.

Most people worry in bits; allowing their worries to come and go during the day. The problem is that they never really get a chance to think their worries through. They worry for a few minutes at a time and then their worrying is interrupted by the telephone or the doorbell or by the need to do something practical — like go to work or get a meal.

The evidence shows that we suffer far less if we allocate thirty minutes a day for worrying. And then make sure that *nothing* interrupts our worrying!

Keep a notebook and a pencil handy and every time something worrying comes into your mind write it down. Unless it's really urgent don't worry about the problem now — wait until your special thirty minute 'worry session' starts. Then, when your personal 'worry session' starts turn off the telephone and go somewhere where you can't hear the doorbell. Make sure that you won't be interrupted. Then concentrate hard on each item that you've put on your list. Try to look at each problem from new angles. Try to see things from other people's point of view.

Most important of all, look at each 'worry' on your list and ask yourself:

'What's the worst that can happen?'

Then look for solutions. Look for answers. Look for ways of dealing with the worries and anxieties you've accumulated.

You'll be amazed! Most of the worries which normally irritate and create tension for days or even weeks can be thought through in an intensive thirty minute 'worry session'.

By concentrating hard on your worries you'll get a chance to put them into perspective. And you'll be surprised how many answers you find and how many problems simply disappear when they're thought about properly.

13. PUT PURPOSE INTO YOUR LIFE

We all need purpose in our lives. We need something to hope for, something to fight for and something to look forward to. Without purpose and meaning your life will be hollow and unrewarding. Purpose and ambition will enable you to live through the worst of life's crises.

Begin putting purpose into your life by making a list of all the goals and ambitions you had when you were a teenager. Try to think back and remember what hopes and aspirations fired your imagination at that age. Then take a look through your list to see just how many of those dreams and ambitions still excite you. You'll probably realise that a number of your old dreams are still within reach.

14. SORT OUT YOUR PRIORITIES

If you fail to differentiate between the big problems and the little ones, and you fail to establish priorities in your life, you will suffer in a number of ways.

First, the number of problems you are exposed to will prove damaging simply because there are so many of them. If you allow yourself to worry about the scratch on your car then your mind will simply add this anxiety to other, more essential worries. Unless you make a conscious decision to separate minor problems from major problems your mind will treat them all in the same way.

Second, while you are worrying about minor irritations you will fail to solve major problems. Getting your priorities sorted out isn't all that difficult. You must decide exactly what is important to you. Try to see things in perspective. Don't be fooled into wasting time on things that are really not important to you. Make a list of the things in your life that are causing you stress. And decide which are really worth worrying about.

15. TIPS TO HELP YOU COPE WITH STRESS

Most doctors only ever tell you about things that you shouldn't do. Here are some things you can do that may revolutionise your life!

1   Say 'I love you' at least once a day to the person you love most in the world. And make sure that they say 'I love you' to you. Those three words make us feel wanted. We live in a world that is too often cruel and thoughtless and full of anger and hatred. Knowing that someone loves you will help protect you against the toxic stress in your life.

2   Spend half a day a week being selfish. Most of us try to cram too much sensible, useful living into our lives. Spend half a day a week doing something that *you* enjoy. Go swimming. Go dancing. Go for a walk. Sit in the park. Have half a day a week that is *yours*.

3   Eat a banana a day. They're better for you than apples. They're cheap and they're absolutely full of fibre and vitamins. But most important of all they come ready wrapped so that when you eat one you don't have to worry about it being contaminated with chemicals or bugs. As a bonus bananas contain few calories — so won't make you fat.

4   Put more fun into your life. Read books that make you laugh. Watch videos that you find truly entertaining. Keep a library of favourite books and videos that you know you can turn to when you're feeling miserable.

5   Stop wasting your life. Throw away any junk mail unopened. Put the phone down on unsolicited,

unwanted calls and shut the door on unsolicited salesmen. In a week you'll save *hours* — enough time to do something you really enjoy. Unsolicited salesmen — usually selling us things we don't want or need — waste an enormous amount of time. And because they're using up your life they're building up your stress.

6 Buy a telephone with an ON-OFF button. And use the OFF button. Or buy a telephone answering machine — and use it to take calls when you want to rest. How many times have you sat down to relax and been disturbed by the phone? How many times have social evenings been interrupted by irrelevant calls? We allow the phone to rule our lives — and we let it get away with rude behaviour that we would never tolerate from children.

7 Keep a diary. You don't have to fill pages with your innermost thoughts. Nor do you have to record tedious, mundane daily happenings. But keeping a diary will help you plan your life more effectively — and therefore avoid many unnecessary and unexpected stresses. A diary will also give you a chance to let off steam in private.

16. TAKE CONTROL OF YOUR LIFE

Ask yourself these four simple but searching questions:

1 How much of your life do you spend doing things to impress people you don't know and whose views and feelings are of no real consequence to you?

2 How much of your life do you spend earning money to buy things you don't really need?

3 Are you doing what you dreamt of doing when you were sixteen?

4 If you died today would you be happy to be remembered for what you have done with your life?

Think carefully about your answers.

The chances are high that up until this moment you have wandered through your life lurching from crisis to crisis; swept along by chance, drifting without aim or purpose and allowing your progress to be determined by accident and fortune.

It is perfectly true that you can't possibly plan every aspect of your life.

Life has a nasty way of hiding surprises for us all.

And even if you could an entirely predictable existence would be flavourless and dull. The unexpected adds spice to life.

But if you want to get the best out of your life you should give yourself some simple goals.

Begin with short term goals.

And ask yourself these simple quesions: *where* do you want to be living, *what* do you want to be doing and *who* do you want to be with in a year's time?

Then move on to medium term goals.

Ask yourself the same three questions.

But with one simple change.

Where do you want to be living, *what* do you want to be doing and *who* do you want to be with in *five years'* time?

Finally, ask yourself *where* you want to be living, *what* you want to be doing and *who* you want to be with in *ten years'* time?

You'll find that if you answer these questions as honestly as you can you will benefit in several ways.

Most importantly, you will have a much clearer idea of what you have to do in order to go at least some of the way towards achieving your aims.

And you will see what steps you need to take in order to live the sort of life you would like to live.

You will also be better prepared to take advantage of the lucky breaks which will inevitably come your way.

Even more important, perhaps, you will be more capable of coping with the bad breaks.

And although many unexpected things will happen to push you from your ideal path through life you will nevertheless have the comfort of knowing that you are going in roughly the direction you want to travel, that you are not wasting your life by meandering along aimlessly and that you have taken some control over your own destiny. You will also have gone a long way towards gaining long term control over your irritable bowel syndrome.

Also published by the European Medical Journal

Mindpower

How to use your mind to heal your body

Vernon Coleman

A new edition of this bestselling manual

- A new approach to health care
- How your mind influences your body
- How to control destructive emotions
- How to deal with guilt
- How to harness positive emotions
- How daydreaming can relax your mind
- How to use your personal strengths
- How to conquer your weaknesses
- How to teach yourself mental self defence
- Specific advice to help you enjoy good health
- •• and much, much more! ••

What they said about the first edition:

☞ Dr Coleman explains the importance of a patient's mental attitude in controlling and treating illness, and suggests some easy-to-learn techniques *Woman's World*

☞ An insight into the most powerful healing agent in the world—the power of the mind *Birmingham Post*

☞ Based on an inspiring message of hope *Western Morning News*

☞ It will be another bestseller *Nursing Times*

ISBN 1 898947 00 7
256pp paperback £9.95

Available from Book Sales, European Medical Journal, PO Box 30, Barnstaple, Devon EX32 9YU. Please write for a catalogue.

Also published by the European Medical Journal

Food for Thought

Your guide to healthy eating

Vernon Coleman

Packed with easy-to-use, up to date, practical information,
Food for Thought is designed to help you differentiate between
fact and fantasy when planning your diet.
The book's 28 chapters include:

- Food the fuel: basic information about carbohydrates, protein, fat, vitamins and minerals
- When water isn't safe to drink—and what to do about it
- How what you eat affects your health
- Why snacking is good for you
- The MINI-MEAL diet and the painless way to lose weight
- Quick tips for losing weight
- The Thirty-Nine Steps to Slenderness
- 20 magic superfoods that can improve your health
- The harm food additives can do
- 20-point plan for avoiding food poisoning
- Drugs and hormones in food
- Food irradiation, genetically altered food, microwaves
- 30 common diseases—and their relationship to what you eat
- How to eat a healthy diet
- 21 reasons for being a vegetarian
- How much should you weigh?
- How to deal with children who are overweight

ISBN 0 9521492 6 5
192pp paperback £9.95

*Available from Book Sales, European Medical Journal,
PO Box 30, Barnstaple, Devon EX32 9YU. Please write for a catalogue.*